Mom,
I Love You

Mom, I Love You

Trudy Booth

PREMIUM PRESS AMERICA
NASHVILLE, TENNESSEE

Mom, I Love You by Trudy Booth
Copyright © 2006

Published by PREMIUM PRESS AMERICA

ISBN 1-887654-54-2
Library of Congress Catalog Number: applied for

PREMIUM PRESS AMERICA gift books are available at special discounts for premiums, sales promotions, fund-raising, or educational use. For details contact the Publisher at P.O. Box 159015, Nashville, TN 37215, or phone toll free (800) 891-7323 or (615) 256-8484, or fax (615) 256-8624.

www.premiumpressamerica.com

Design by Armour&Armour, Nashville, Tennessee
www.armour-armour.com

First Edition April 2006
1 2 3 4 5 6 7 8 9 10

To the mothers
of the world

My mother is a poem
I'll never be able to write,
though everything I write
is a poem to my mother.

Sharon Doubiago

A Mother Is . . .

A mother is she who can take the place of all others, but whose place no one else can take.

Cardinal Mermillod

The moment a child is born, the mother is also born. She never existed before. The woman existed, but the mother, never. A mother is something absolutely new.

Rajneesh

Mothers are the pivot on
which the family spins,
Mothers are the pivot on
which the world spins.

Pam Brown

2

Mother is the one we count on for the things that matter most of all.

Katherine Butler Hathaway

A Mother's Prayer

Hope

DEAR FATHER in Heaven, I come to You today with my heart full of hope. I look into the faces of my children, and I see bright promises of the future. I feel the reassurance of Your universe unfolding as they boldly step forward to shape the world according to Your purpose. Father, let me share my hope with them, and let them rest knowing that You will walk with them and care for them.

The Magic Word

To a child's ear, mother is
magic in any language.
Arlene Benedict

So when the great word "Mother!" rang once
more, I saw at last its meaning and its place;
Not the blind passion of the brooding past,
But Mother—the World's Mother—come at
last, To love as she had never loved before—To
feed and guard and teach the human race.
Charlotte Perkins Gilman

Mother: the most beautiful word
on the lips of mankind.
Kahil Gibran

My Mother

ABRAHAM LINCOLN

Nancy Hanks Lincoln, trained as a seamstress, was known for her hard work, cheerfulness, and intelligence. She was ambitious for her children and wanted them to have opportunities she and her husband had missed out on. She drank bad milk when Abe was nine years old. She called her children to her deathbed and urged them to be kind to their father, to each other, and to the world.

Lincoln later said, "All that I am or ever hope to be, I owe to my angel Mother. I remember my mother's prayers and they have always followed me. They have clung to me all my life."

Motherhood is like
Albania: You can't trust
the brochures; you
have to go there.

Marni Jackson

The Lighter Side of Moms

Children are a great comfort in your old
age—and they help you reach it faster, too.

Lionel Kauffman

Insanity is hereditary; you get
it from your children.

Sam Levenson

The one thing children wear out
faster than shoes is parents.

John J. Plomp

If evolution really works, how come
mothers only have two hands?

Milton Berle

Mother Love

The mother love is like God's love; he loves us not because we are lovable, but because it is His nature to love, and because we are His children.

Earl Riney

God sees us through our mothers' eyes and rewards us for our virtues.

Ganeshan Venkatarman

There is a religion in all deep love, but the love of a mother is the veil of a softer light between the heart and the heavenly Father.

Samuel Taylor Coleridge

Mother love is the
fuel that enables
a normal human
being to do the
impossible.

Marion C. Garretty

There shall never be another quite so tender, quite
so kind as the patient little mother, nowhere on
this earth you'll find her affection duplicated.
Paul C. Brownlow

A mother laughs our laughter,
Sheds our tears,
Returns our love,
Fears our fears.
She lives our joys,
Cares our cares,
And all our hopes and dreams she shares.
Julia Summers

Potpourri

MOTHER'S DAY BY THE NUMBERS

- $10.43 billion   Amount spent on Mother's Day

- $868 million   Amount spent on flowers

- $98.64   Average amount spent per consumer

- $62.40   Average amount spent on jewelry

- $40.54   Average amount spent on dining out

- $31.89   Average amount spent on clothing

Mom, the Teacher

Children are the sum of what mothers
contribute to their lives.

Unknown

I long to put the experience of fifty years at once
into your young lives, to give you at once the key
of that treasure chamber every gem of which has
cost me tears and struggles and prayers, but you
must work for these inward treasures yourself.

Harriet Beecher Stowe

For the mother is and must be, whether she
knows it or not, the greatest, strongest and
most lasting teacher her children have.

Hannah W. Smith

There was never
a great man
who had not a
great mother.

Olive Schreiner

My Mother

THOMAS EDISON

When a schoolmaster called him "addled," his furious mother took Thomas Edison out of the school and proceeded to teach him at home. He said many years later, "My mother was the making of me. She was so true, so sure of me, and I felt I had some one to live for, some one I must not disappoint."

Making the decision
to have a child—it's
momentous. It is to
decide forever to have
your heart go walking
around outside your body.

Elizabeth Stone

Potpourri

MOTHERS BY THE NUMBERS

- **10%**   Percentage of women who end their childbearing years with four or more children.

- **3**   Average number of children that women in Utah and Alaska can expect to have in their lifetime.

- **2**   Average number of children that women in the U.S. today can expect to have in their lifetime.

- **4 million**   Number of women who have babies each year.

- **425,000**   Number of teens, ages 15 to 19, who have babies each year.

- **100,000**   Number of women age 40 or over who have babies each year.

Reflections

Motherhood is the greatest potential influence in human society. Her caress first awakens in the child a sense of security; her kiss the first realization of affection; her sympathy and tenderness, the first assurance that there is love in the world. Thus in infancy and childhood she implants ever-directing and restraining influences that remain through life.

David O. McKay

A Mother's Prayer

Love

DEAR HEAVENLY Father, what perfect love you have opened to me—the love a mother has for her child. Surely, it is as close to divinity as any gift we have on Earth. Thank You for sharing the blessing of motherhood with me, and forgive me when I fall short in setting the right example for my children. Guide my thoughts, words, and actions, that I might know how to guide them.

When it comes to love,
mom's the word.

Author Unknown

The Power of Love

No language can express the power and
beauty and heroism of a mother's love.
Edwin H. Chapin

A mother's love for her child is like nothing
else in the world. It knows no law, no
pity, it dares all things and crushes down
remorselessly all that stands in its path.
Agatha Christie

A mother's love perceives no impossibilities.
Cornelia Paddock

Potpourri

MOTHERS BY THE NUMBERS

- **25.1**   Average age of women when they give birth for the first time

- **40%**   Percentage of births annually that are the mother's first

- **1 in 32**   Odds of a woman delivering twins

- **1 in 540** Odds of a woman having triplets or other multiple births

- **August** The most popular month in which to have a baby, with 359,000 births

- **July**   The second most popular month, with 358,000

- **Tuesday** The most popular day of the week to have a baby

I think my life began with waking
up and loving my mother's face.

George Eliot

Of all the joys that brighten suffering earth,
what joy is welcomed like a newborn child?

Caroline Norton

Youth fades; love droops,
the leaves of friendship fall;
A mother's secret hope outlives them all.

Oliver Wendell Holmes

Where Love Resides

A mother's heart is always with her children.

Proverb

My mother had a slender, small body,
but a large heart—a heart so large that
everybody's joys found welcome in it,
and hospitable accommodation.

Mark Twain

A mother's heart is a beautiful
expression of God's everlasting love.

Author Unknown

Sweater, n.:
garment worn
by child when
its mother is
feeling chilly.

Ambrose Bierce

Working Hand in Hand

As a mother my job is to take care
of the possible and trust God
with the impossible.

Ruth Bell Graham

God could not be everywhere
and therefore he made mothers.

Jewish proverb

Mothers reflect God's
loving presence on Earth.

William R. Webb

Reflections

M aybe children should come
with instructions.

Until you become a mother, you don't
realize how different each child can
be. You can't take the same approach
for each child. A tactic that worked
with your oldest child doesn't work
with the second child. And by the
time you have the third child, you
don't make a plan.

You just wing it and try to look good
in the process.

You can fool all of the people some of the time, and some of the people all of the time, but you Can't Fool Mom.

Captain Penny's Law

Sometimes the poorest woman leaves
her children the richest inheritance.
Ruth E. Renkel

Of all the rights of women, the
greatest is to be a mother.
Lin Yutang

She made me a security blanket when
I was born. That faded green blanket
lasted just long enough for me to realize
that the security part came from her.
Alexander Crane

My Mother

LOUISA MAY ALCOTT

Louisa May Alcott, author of *Little Women*, began her writing to support her perpetually impoverished family. Her strong and loving mother was a significant force in her life. "I think she is a very brave, good woman," Alcott wrote of her mother. "And my dream is to have a lovely, quiet home for her, with no debts or troubles to burden her."

Teach Your Children Well

The mother's heart is the child's schoolroom.
Henry Ward Beecher

You may have tangible wealth untold;
Caskets of jewels and coffers of gold.
Richer than I you can never be—
I had a mother who read to me.
Strickland Gillilan

One good mother is worth a
hundred schoolmasters.
George Herbert

My mother could make anybody feel guilty. She used to get letters of apology from people she didn't even know.

Joan Rivers

More Mom Humor

Always be nice to your children because they are the ones who will choose your rest home.
Phyllis Diller

Why do grandparents and grandchildren get along so well? They have the same enemy—the mother.
Claudette Colbert

My mother's menu consisted of two choices: take it or leave it.
Buddy Hackett

Motherhood

> Motherhood: All love
> begins and ends there.
> ### *Robert Browning*

> The strength of motherhood
> is greater than natural laws.
> ### *Barbara Kingsolver*

> Mighty is the force of
> motherhood! It transforms
> all things by its vital heat.
> ### *George Eliot*

Reflections

Motherhood is the one thing in all the world which most truly exemplifies the God-given virtues of creating and sacrificing. Though it carries the woman close to the brink of death, motherhood also leads her into the very realm of the fountains of life, and makes her co-partner with the Creator in bestowing upon eternal spirits mortal life.

David O. McKay

A Mother Is . . .

A mother is one to whom you
hurry when you are troubled.
Emily Dickinson

A mother is someone who dreams
great dreams for you, but then she lets
you chase the dreams you have for
yourself and loves you just the same.
Author Unknown

A mother is the only person on Earth who
can divide her love among ten children
and each child still have all her love.
Author Unknown

Mothers are the most
instinctive philosophers.
Harriet Beecher Stowe

Mothers all want their sons to grow up
to be president, but they don't want them
to become politicians in the process.
John Fitzgerald Kennedy

All that I am my mother made me.
John Quincy Adams

With what price we pay for the
glory of motherhood.

Isadora Duncan

A Mother's Prayer

Joy

MY LORD, when I see the wonder of the child You have created, the joy in my heart overflows. His smile can lighten the heaviest heart; his laughter brings music into the dullest day. When I look at the face of Your miraculous child, I see Your glory brought to life. Thank You, Lord, for sharing with me the bliss of being a mother.

A Mother's Heart . . .

The heart of a mother is a deep
abyss at the bottom of which you
will always find forgiveness.
Honoré de Balzac

Mother is the heartbeat in the
home; and without her, there
seems to be no heart throb.
Leroy Brownlow

A mother's heart is a patchwork of love.
Author Unknown

Who ran to help me when I fell,
And would some pretty story tell,
Or kiss the place to make it well?
My mother.

Ann Taylor

Mother—that was the bank where we
deposited all our hurts and worries.

T. DeWitt Talmage

The real religion of the world comes
from women much more than from
men—from mothers most of all, who carry
the key of our souls in their bosoms.

Oliver Wendell Holmes

No matter how
old a mother is,
she watches her
middle-aged
children for signs
of improvement.

Florida Scott-Maxwell

A Mother's Prayer

Wisdom

DEAR HEAVENLY Father, I humbly come before You today asking for the guidance of Your wisdom. Show me how to live my life in such a way that my child will be a glory to You. Help me to know the lessons to teach and the steps to take, to lead my child in the path of Your light. Let my knowledge and actions come from Your divine inspiration, the source of all true wisdom.

There are lots of things that you can
brush under the carpet about yourself
until you're faced with somebody
whose needs won't be put off.
Angela Carter

Parents often talk about the
younger generation as if they didn't
have anything to do with it.
Haim Ginott

I never thought that you should be
rewarded for the greatest privilege of life.
Mary Roper Coker

Mother is the name for
God on the lips and in the
hearts of little children.

William Makepeace Thackeray

Safe in the Arms of Love

Mother's arms are made of tenderness, and
sweet sleep blesses the child who lies therein.

Victor Hugo

The story of a mother's life: Trapped
between a scream and a hug.

Cathy Guisewite

No one hugs like mom!

Author Unknown

Reflections

Every day of motherhood brings new experiences and challenges. You never know what to expect from one day to the next. That's the fun part.

You can't imagine who is going to fall and get hurt, or who is going to forget and leave their lunchbox on the table. Times like that are when you shine. You do what is necessary to save the day—and guess what your reward is? To hear your child say, "Thanks, Mom. I love you."

What can be better than that?

Before I got
married I had six
theories about
bringing up
children; now I
have six children,
and no theories.

John Wilmot

A Mother's Love

Some are kissing mothers and
some are scolding mothers, but it
is love just the same—and most
mothers kiss and scold together.

Pearl S. Buck

Mother's love grows by giving.

Charles Lamb

Rejecting things because they are old-
fashioned would rule out the sun and
the moon, and a mother's love.

Author Unknown

The Oldest Profession

The phrase working mother is redundant.
Jane Sellman

I looked on child-rearing not only as a work
of love and duty but as a profession that was
fully as interesting and challenging as any
honorable profession in the world and one
that demanded the best that I could bring it.
Rose Kennedy

Being a full-time mother is one of
the highest salaried jobs . . . since
the payment is pure love.
Mildred B. Vermont

Being a mother
is learning about
strengths you didn't
know you had ... and
dealing with fears you
didn't know existed.

Linda Wooten

And so our mothers and grandmothers have,
more often than not unknown, handed on
the creative spark, the seed of the flower
they themselves never hoped to see—or like
a sealed letter they could not plainly read.

Alice Walker

You don't really understand human
nature unless you know why a child
on a merry-go-round will wave at his
parents every time around—and why
his parents will always wave back.

William D. Tammeus

The Power of Mom

The hand that rocks the cradle is
the hand that rules the world.

W. S. Ross

To be a mother is a woman's greatest vocation
in life. She is a partner with God. No being
has a position of such power and influence.
She holds in her hands the destiny of nations,
for to her comes the responsibility and
opportunity of molding the nation's citizens.

Spencer W. Kimball

To describe my mother would be to write
about a hurricane in its perfect power.

Maya Angelou

How to Raise a Child

If you want your children to turn out
well, spend twice as much time with
them, and half as much money.

Abigail Van Buren

Women know
The way to rear up children (to be just)
They know a simple, merry, tender knack
Of tying sashes, fitting baby shoes,
And stringing pretty words that make no sense,
And kissing full sense into empty words.

Elizabeth Barrett Browning

What good mothers and fathers instinctively feel
like doing for their babies is usually best after all.

Dr. Benjamin Spock

My mother had
a great deal of
trouble with
me, but I think
she enjoyed it.

Mark Twain

Reflections

Before you become a mother, you never realize how much children enrich your life. It is a feeling that you can't explain unless you are a mother.

You have a sense of responsibility that does not carry weight, but instead carries a joy of the blessing that you were given. And when you look into your children's eyes, you realize not only are they your joy, but you are theirs, too.

So cherish each moment you have with your children, because one day they will grow up.

You don't
appreciate your
mother until you're
a mother yourself.

Catherine Pulsifer

Unconditional Love

Who is it that loves me and will love me
forever with an affection which no chance,
no misery, no crime of mine can do away?
It is you, my mother.

Thomas Carlyle

A mother loves her children even
when they least deserve to be loved.

Kate Samperi

A father may turn his back on his
child, brothers and sisters may become
inveterate enemies, husbands may desert
their wives, wives their husbands. But
a mother's love endures through all.

Washington Irving

Family Life

Woman knows what man has long forgotten,
that the ultimate economic and spiritual
unit of any civilization is still the family.
Clare Boothe Luce

Good family life is never an accident but
always an achievement by those who share it.
James H. Bossard

I don't care how poor a man is;
if he has family, he's rich.
Colonel Sherman Potter, "M*A*S*H"

It is not what you do for
your children but what
you have taught them
to do for themselves
that will make them
successful human beings.

Ann Landers

To the world you might just be one person,
but to one person you might just be the world.
Author Unknown

Oh, the comfort, the inexpressible comfort
of feeling safe with a person, having
neither to weigh thoughts nor measure
words, but pouring them all out, just as
they are, chaff and grain together, certain
that a faithful hand will take and sift them,
keep what is worth keeping, and with a
breath of kindness blow the rest away.
George Eliot

Words of Wisdom

To understand a mother's love, you
must raise children yourself.

Chinese Proverb

A man loves his sweetheart the most, his
wife the best, but his mother the longest.

Irish Proverb

There is only one pretty child in the
world, and every mother has it.

Ancient Proverb

A mother understands what
a child does not say.

Jewish Proverb

A mother is a person who, seeing there are only four pieces of pie for five people, promptly announces she never did care for pie.

Tenneva Jordan

My Mother

GEORGE WASHINGTON

George Washington, the father of our country, always said he owed his success to his mother. His father died when he was only 11, and George became head of the household. He and his mother raised the family and managed a 600-acre farm. Deeply religious and reportedly strict, she often read to her children from her favorite book of maxims, a book George kept with him all his life.

"All I am I owe to my mother," George said. "I attribute all my success in life to the moral, intellectual and physical education I received from her."

Mama exhorted her children at every opportunity to "jump at de sun." We might not land on the sun, but at least we would get off the ground.

Zora Neale Hurston

A Mother's Prayer
Patience

HEAVENLY FATHER, as I guide my children today, help me to remember the patience You show to me in the face of my shortcomings. Soften my heart when my babies misbehave, and grant me the wisdom to nurture them when they stray. Let me be led by perfect love for You and for them. Forgive me when I stumble, and help me walk in a way they will be proud to follow.

The Empty Nest

It will be gone before you know it. The fingerprints
on the wall appear higher and higher.
Then suddenly they disappear.

Dorothy Evslin

It kills you to see them grow up. But I guess
it would kill you quicker if they didn't.

Barbara Kingsolver

When mothers talk about the depression of the empty
nest, they're not mourning the passing of all those
wet towels on the floor, or the music that numbs your
teeth, or even the bottle of capless shampoo dribbling
down the shower drain. They're upset because they've
gone from supervisor of a child's life to a spectator.

Erma Bombeck

The Bottomless Heart

With every child, your heart grows bigger
and stronger—that there is no limit to how
much or how many people you can love, even
though at times you feel as though you could
burst—you don't—you just love even more.

Yasmin Le Bon

You never realize how much your mother loves
you till you explore the attic—and find every
letter you ever sent her, every finger painting,
clay pot, bead necklace, Easter chicken,
cardboard Santa Claus, paperlace Mother's
Day card and school report since day one.

Pam Brown

The first Mother's Day

Julia Ward Howe first introduced the idea of Mother's Day in 1870. She conceived it as a day for women to advocate pacifism and disarmament.

Early celebrations were sponsored by women's peace groups. They often hosted meetings of mothers whose sons had died fighting on opposite sides of the Civil War.

Her Special Day

Mother's Day is in honor of the best mother
who ever lived—the mother of your heart.

Anna Jarvis

Spend at least one Mother's Day with your
respective mothers before you decide on marriage.

Erma Bombeck

The only mothers it is safe to forget on
Mother's Day are the good ones.

Mignon McLaughlin

Recipes for Mothers

When God thought of mother, He must
have laughed with satisfaction, and
framed it quickly—so rich, so deep,
so divine, so full of soul, power, and
beauty, was the conception.

Henry Ward Beecher

Her dignity consists in being unknown
to the world; her glory is in the esteem
of her husband; her pleasures in the
happiness of her family.

Jean Rousseau

Reflections

A MOTHER'S RECIPE

1 heart of love
2 cups of laughter
2 ½ cups of patience
A bundle of hugs and kisses
An indefinite amount of energy

Take and mix the love and laughter together thoroughly. Once they have been mixed well, start sprinkling in the patience. You will need it once you leave the kitchen and see the rest of the house. Start folding in hugs and kisses to show your kids that you still love them. Each day after, start putting in handsful of energy because you will need more and more as the days progress.

The Miracle of Birth

Bringing a child into the world is
the greatest act of hope there is.

Louise Hart

Now the thing about having a baby—and
I can't be the first person to have noticed
this—is that thereafter you have it.

Jean Kerr

Childbirth is more admirable than
conquest, more amazing than self-defense,
and as courageous as either one.

Gloria Steinem

A suburban
mother's role is to
deliver children
obstetrically
once, and by car
forever after.

Peter de Vries

Reflections

The other day I decided to run away. Me, the mother—not the child.

The kids were aggravating each other, the baby was crying, and on top of all that, I was tired. So I decided to run away.

Then I had to think, what would happen to my family? The kids wouldn't have a referee for their fights; the baby wouldn't have anyone to cry to; Daddy wouldn't know the first thing about picking out the kids' clothes or cooking dinner; and most of all, I wouldn't have anyone to love. So I thought it over and decided that, even though time without constant bickering, crying, and being asked "what's for dinner" sounds good, nothing beats hearing your family tell you they love you.

Erica Dailey

National Mother's Day

In 1907 Anna Jarvis celebrated a private Mother's Day to mark the anniversary of her mother's death. Her mother, also Anna Jarvis, had participated in Julia Ward Howe's Mother's Day celebrations for peace.

Anna the daughter was determined to make Mother's Day a national event. Her campaign, financed by clothing merchant John Wanamaker, succeeded in 1910 when West Virginia was the first state to officially recognize the holiday.

President Woodrow Wilson proclaimed Mother's Day a national holiday in 1914.

In the 1920s Anna filed suit to protect her holiday from commercialization. She failed, and Mother's Day is now a billion-dollar industry.

Maternity is on the face of it an unsociable experience. The selfishness that a woman has learned to stifle or to dissemble where she alone is concerned, blooms freely and unashamed on behalf of her offspring.

Emily James Putnam

A woman has two smiles that an angel might envy, the smile that accepts a lover before words are uttered, and the smile that lights on the first-born babe, and assures it of a mother's love.

Thomas C. Haliburton

Motherhood is
full of frustrations
and challenges, but
eventually they
move out.

Author Unknown

A mother holds
her children's
hands for a
while, their
hearts forever.

Author Unknown

A Mother's Prayer

Thanksgiving

DEAR LORD, You have filled my life with a blessing greater than I ever knew existed: my precious child. Thank You for creating the miracle of life, this child with sparkling eyes, strong fingers, and sturdy legs. Thank You for choosing me, Lord, for entrusting me with this treasure valued above all others. With Your strength and guidance, I devote myself to rearing my child as a reflection of Your glory.

Listen to your Mother!

Sooner or later we all quote our mothers.
Bern Williams

When your mother asks, "Do you want
a piece of advice?" it's a mere formality.
It doesn't matter if you answer yes or
no. You're going to get it anyway.
Erma Bombeck

By the time a woman realizes that maybe
her mother was right, she has a daughter
who thinks everything she does is wrong.
Author Unknown

Every beetle
is a gazelle
in the eyes
of its mother.

Moorish Proverb

Potpourri

MOTHERS IN SONG

- "My Mama Said"   ABBA

- "Mother and Child Reunion"   Paul Simon

- "Mother's Pride"   George Michael

- "Mother"   John Lennon

- "Mama's Always on Stage"   Arrested Development

- "Mamas, Don't Let Your Babies
  Grow up to be Cowboys"   Waylon Jennings

- "Mother"   Tori Amos

- "Dear Mama"   Tupac Shakur

They're Playing her Song

M is for the million things she gave me,
O means only that she's growing old,
T is for the tears she shed to save me,
H is for her heart of purest gold;
E is for her eyes, with love-light shining,
R means right, and right she'll always be,
Put them all together, they spell MOTHER,
A word that means the world to me.

Howard Johnson

Because I feel that in the heavens above
The angels, whispering one to another,
Can find among their burning tears of love,
None so devotional as that of Mother,
Therefore, by that dear name
I have long called you, You who are
more than mother unto me.

Edgar Allan Poe

Bitter are the tears of a child: Sweeten them.
Deep are the thoughts of a child: Quiet them.
Sharp is the grief of a child: Take it from him.
Soft is the heart of a child: Do not harden it.

Pamela Glenconner

Potpourri

MOTHERS BY THE NUMBERS

- 82.5 million   Estimated number of mothers of all ages in the U.S.

- 68%   Percentage of women in Mississippi, ages 15 to 44, who are mothers.

- 56%   Percentage of women in the U.S., ages 15 to 44, who are mothers.

- 82%   Percentage of women, ages 40 to 44, who are mothers.

Teach Your Children Well

That best academy, a mother's knee.
James Russell Lowell

If you bungle raising your children,
I don't think whatever else you
do matters very much!
Jacqueline Kennedy Onassis

Each day of our lives we make deposits
in the memory banks of our children.
Charles R. Swindoll

The mother is queen of that realm
and sways a scepter more potent
than that of kings or priests.
Author Unknown

The mother of three notoriously unruly youngsters was asked whether or not she'd have children if had it to do over again. "Sure," she replied. "But not the same ones."

Author Unknown

A Mother's Prayer

Peace

DEAR LORD, I come to You today looking for the peace and solace of Your arms. As the world around me buzzes by, I look to You for a garden of quiet. Thank You, Lord, for renewing my soul and replenishing my stability. Thank You for giving me a peaceful heart as I walk in a frantic world.

The precursor of the mirror
is the mother's face.
D.W. Winnicott

I am convinced that while people keep the
memory of their mothers' loving faces alive
in their minds, they will never go far astray.
Daisaku Ikeda

The most important thing a father can do
for his children is to love their mother.
Henry Ward Beecher

Reflections

The love of a mother goes beyond the simple phrase, "I love you." It is the kind of love that may go unseen, except to your children.

A mother's love shows when you put your child in time-out for misbehaving. It shows when you take your child to the park just to enjoy feeding the ducks. And most of all, it shows when your child is in your arms and the two of you share a big hug.

The unconditional love you bring your family is more powerful than all the bad behaviors and quirky habits that drive you up the wall.

Support

A mother is the one who is still there
when everyone else has deserted you.
Author Unknown

I cannot forget my mother. She is
my bridge. When I needed to get
across, she steadied herself long
enough for me to run across safely.
Renita Weems

One of the oldest human needs is having
someone to wonder where you are
when you don't come home at night.
Margaret Mead

Biology is the least of what
makes someone a mother.

Oprah Winfrey

Motherhood is neither a duty nor a privilege,
but simply the way that humanity can
satisfy the desire for physical immortality
and triumph over the fear of death.

Rebecca West

Motherhood is priced of God,
at price no man may dare
To lessen or misunderstand.

Helen Hunt Jackson

She never quite leaves
her children at home,
even when she doesn't
take them along.

Margaret Culkin Banning

The Oldest Profession

Nobody knows of the work it makes
To keep the home together.
Nobody knows of the steps it takes,
Nobody knows—but Mother.

Nancy Thayer

Motherhood: If it were going to
be easy, it never would have started
with something called labor.

Barbara Johnson

If at first you don't
succeed, do it like your
mother told you.

Author Unknown

Home Sweet Home

What is home without a mother?
Alice Hawthorne

Where we love is home—home that
our feet may leave, but not our hearts.
Oliver Wendell Holmes Sr.

Mom, when thoughts of you are in our
hearts, we are never far from home.
Author Unknown

A little girl, asked where her home
was, replied, where mother is.
Keith L. Brooks

I love these little people; and it is
not a slight thing, when they, who
are so fresh from God, love us.

Charles Dickens

A grandmother is a mother
who has a second chance.

Author Unknown

A mother's happiness is like a beacon,
lighting up the future but reflected also on
the past in the guise of fond memories.

Honoré de Balzac

Working Mothers

All mothers are working mothers.
Author Unknown

By and large, mothers and housewives are the
only workers who do not have regular time
off. They are the great vacationless class.
Anne Morrow Lindbergh

Any mother could perform the jobs of
several air traffic controllers with ease.
Lisa Alther

Now, as always, the most automated
appliance in a household is the mother.
Beverly Jones

When you are a mother, you are never really alone in your thoughts. A mother always has to think twice, once for herself and once for her child.

Sophia Loren

Mothers have to remember what food each child likes or dislikes, which one is allergic to penicillin and hamster fur, who gets carsick and who isn't kidding when he stands outside the bathroom door and tells you what's going to happen if he doesn't get in right away. It's tough. If they all have the same hair color, they tend to run together.

Erma Bombeck

Reflections

The noblest calling in the world is that of mother. True motherhood is the most beautiful of all arts, the greatest of all professions. She who can paint a masterpiece or who can write a book that will influence millions deserves the plaudits and admiration of mankind; but she who rears successfully a family of healthy, beautiful sons and daughters whose immortal souls will be exerting an influence throughout the ages long after paintings shall have faded, and books and statues shall have been destroyed, deserves the highest honor that man can give.

David O. McKay

A mother is not
a person to lean
on, but a person
to make leaning
unnecessary.

Dorothy Canfield Fisher

Together Forever

Children and mothers never truly part—
Bound in the beating of each other's heart.
Charlotte Gray

And it came to me, and I knew what I had
to have before my soul would rest. I wanted
to belong—to belong to my mother. And in
return—I wanted my mother to belong to me.
Gloria Vanderbilt

The tie which links mother and
child is of such pure and immaculate
strength as to be never violated.
Washington Irving

Nothing else will ever make you as happy or as sad, as proud or as tired, as motherhood.

Elia Parsons

In God's great
vaudeville,
Mother is the
headliner.

Elbert Hubbard

More Mom Humor

Setting a good example for your children
takes all the fun out of middle age.
William Feather

It is not a bad thing that children
should occasionally, and politely,
put parents in their place.
Author Unknown

The best way to keep children home is to
make the home atmosphere pleasant—
and let the air out of the tires.
Dorothy Parker

Potpourri

CLASSIC MOMS ON TV

The Fifties

Character	Show	Played by
Lucy Ricardo	"I Love Lucy"	Lucille Ball
June Cleaver	"Leave It To Beaver"	Barbara Billingsley
Harriet Nelson	"Ozzie and Harriet"	Harriet Nelson
Margaret Anderson	"Father Knows Best"	Jane Wyatt
Donna Stone	"The Donna Reed Show"	Donna Reed

The Sixties

Laura Petrie	"The Dick Van Dyke Show"	Mary Tyler Moore
Dr. Maureen Robinson	"Lost in Space"	June Lockhart
Morticia Addams	"The Addams Family"	Carolyn Jones
Lily Munster	"The Munsters"	Yvonne De Carlo
Kate Bradley	"Petticoat Junction"	Bea Benaderet
Carol Brady	"The Brady Bunch"	Florence Henderson
Gladys Crabtree	"My Mother the Car"	Ann Sothern
Samantha Stevens	"Bewitched"	Elizabeth Montgomery

The Weaker Sex

It's not easy being a mother. If it
were easy, fathers would do it.
Dorothy Zbornak, "The Golden Girls"

Women's Liberation is just a lot of
foolishness. It's the men who are
discriminated against. They can't
bear children. And no one's likely
to do anything about that.

Golda Meir

If nature had arranged that husbands and
wives should have children alternatively, there
would never be more than three in a family.

Lawrence Housman

When I pick up one of my children and
cuddle them, all the strain and stress of life
temporarily disappears. There is nothing more
wonderful than motherhood and no one
will ever love you as much as a small child.

Nicola Horlick

If a man gives his mother a gift
certificate for a flu shot, dump him.

Erma Bombeck

No influence is so powerful
as that of the mother.

Sarah Josepha Hale

I'm Not Going to Tell You Again!

Kids really brighten a household.
They never turn off the lights.

Ralph Bus

Have you any idea how many
children it takes to turn off one
light in the kitchen? Three. It takes
one to say, "What light?" and two
more to say, "I didn't turn it on."

Erma Bombeck

When a woman is twenty,
a child deforms her;

when she is thirty,
he preserves her;

and when forty, he
makes her young again.

Leon Blum

R-E-S-P-E-C-T

If a mother respects both herself and her child from his very first day onward, she will never need to teach him respect for others.

Alice Miller

One of the very few reasons I had any respect for my mother when I was thirteen was because she would reach into the sink with her bare hands—bare hands—and pick up that lethal gunk and drop it into the garbage. To top that, I saw her reach into the wet garbage bag and fish around in there looking for a lost teaspoon. Bare hands—a kind of mad courage.

Robert Fulghum

A Mother Knows You Best

A mother understands when no one else can!
Author Unknown

Life is the fruit she longs to hand you,
Ripe on a plate.
And while you live,
Relentlessly she understands you.
Phyllis McGinley

A mother's first gift is life, the second is
love, and the third is understanding.
Author Unknown

Mothers are like opinions. Everybody has one, and everybody thinks theirs is the best!
Christopher Armour

A woman with a child rediscovers the world. All is changed—politics, loyalties, needs. For now all is judged by the life of the child . . . and of all children.

Pam Brown

Grown don't mean nothing to a mother. A child is a child. They get bigger, older, but grown? What's that suppose to mean? In my heart it don't mean a thing.
Toni Morrison

Motherhood

There is no greater good in all the world than
motherhood. The influence of a mother in the
lives of her children is beyond calculation.

James E. Faust

Oh what a power is motherhood,
possessing a potent spell!

Euripedes

Motherhood has a very humanizing effect.
Everything gets reduced to essentials.

Meryl Streep

My Mother

JANET RENO

Janet Reno rose to become the first female attorney general for the United States. Her childhood taught her to strive for excellence as well as stand for absolute honesty. Her mother, a journalist, built the family's home and was known to wrestle alligators. Significantly, her mother influenced her with this homily: "Good, better, best. Don't ever rest until good is better and better is best."

A Mother's Love

Who is it that loves me and will love
me forever with an affection which no
chance, no misery, no crime of mine
can do away? It is you, my mother.

Thomas Carlyle

The mother loves her child most divinely, not
when she surrounds him with comfort and
anticipates his wants but when she resolutely
holds him to the highest standards and is
content with nothing less than his best.

Hamilton W. Mabie

Reflections

As a child growing up, your list to Santa starts in July. You bug your mother day in and day out about getting the address to the North Pole. Of course, as the mother, you know you are Santa and that letter to the North Pole goes in the dresser drawer where kids are not allowed. You keep that secret until one of their friends tells them differently.

That is the goodness of motherhood, knowing how to take a backseat even when you deserve all the credit.

Mothers and Sons

Men are what their mothers made them.
Ralph Waldo Emerson

He is a poor son whose sonship
does not make him desire
to serve all men's mothers.
Harry Emerson Fosdick

No man succeeds without a
good woman behind him.
Wife or mother, if it is both,
he is twice blessed indeed.
Harold MacMillan

Mothers And Daughters

When I stopped seeing my mother with
the eyes of a child, I saw the woman
who helped me give birth to myself.

Nancy Friday

A daughter is a mother's gender partner,
her closest ally in the family confederacy,
an extension of her self. And mothers
are their daughters' role model, their
biological and emotional road map,
the arbiter of all their relationships.

Victoria Secunda

All women
become like their
mothers. That
is their tragedy.
No man does.
That's his.

Oscar Wilde

A Mother is . . .

Never being number one in your list
of priorities and not minding at all.

Jasmine Guinness

A mother is the truest friend we have,
when trials, heavy and sudden, fall upon
us; when adversity takes the place of
prosperity; when friends who rejoice with
us in our sunshine, desert us; when troubles
thicken around us, still will she cling to
us, and endeavor by her kind precepts and
counsels to dissipate the clouds of darkness,
and cause peace to return to our hearts.

Washington Irving

Premium Gift Books from PREMIUM PRESS AMERICA include:

I'LL BE DOGGONE
CATS OUT OF THE BAG

GREAT AMERICAN CIVIL WAR
GREAT AMERICAN GOLF
GREAT AMERICAN OUTDOORS
GREAT AMERICAN GUIDE TO FINE WINES
GREAT AMERICAN WOMEN

ANGELS EVERYWHERE
MIRACLES
SNOW ANGELS
POWER OF PRAYER
GOLDEN TRUTHS, OLD TESTAMENT

ABSOLUTELY ALABAMA
AMAZING ARKANSAS
FABULOUS FLORIDA
GORGEOUS GEORGIA
SENSATIONAL SOUTH CAROLINA
TERRIFIC TENNESSEE
TREMENDOUS TEXAS
VINTAGE VIRGINIA
MIGHTY MISSISSIPPI

TITANTIC TRIVIA
BILL DANCE'S FISHING TIPS
DREAM CATCHERS
STORY KEEPERS
AMERICA THE BEAUTIFUL
STORY OF GATLINBURG

PREMIUM PRESS AMERICA routinely updates existing titles and frequently adds new topics to its growing line of premium gift books. Books are distributed through gift and specialty shops, and bookstores nationwide. If, for any reason, books are not available in your area, please contact the local distributor listed above or contact the Publisher direct by calling 1-800-891-7323. To see our complete backlist and current books, you can visit our website at *www.premiumpressamerica.com*. Thank you.

Great Reading. Premium Gifts